About the author

Lola R. Opeyemi was born in Nigeria and has lived in London, Amsterdam and Kampala.
She is a keen travel and architectural enthusiast and will travel pretty much anywhere for food and pretty buildings.

If you liked my book, please leave a review & tell your friends.

Love,
Lola
xoxo

First published in 2023 by Spoken Tree Writing Company.

For permission requests, please write to the publisher at the email address below:
mail@lolaropeyemi.com

This novel is a work of narrative non-fiction. Names have been altered to protect the identity of the people involved.

Paperback ISBN: 978 1 838107437

Thank you to God for this book.

The Music of Water – an African Travelogue

This is a work of narrative non-fiction. Names have been altered to protect the identity of the people involved.

Part 1: Kenya, Mozambique and Tanzania

Kenya

The Orphanage

Apart from Nigeria, where I was born and raised, I have never been to any countries in Africa.

I dreamed of faraway places like Kenya, but I assumed my meagre means would never get me there.

My first foray into Africa came in December 2016, when I planned a trip to two countries: Mozambique and Tanzania with a connecting flight in Kenya.

Cadette, my travel companion, and I decided to hit cities only because… well, we were city girls.

We were all set to go to Maputo and Dar Es Salaam when the airline emailed saying, the connection from Nairobi to Maputo could no longer be honoured, did we want to change to another day or spend an overnight in Kenya – with all costs covered by the airline. It was a no-brainer. We could hit three countries in two weeks instead of two.

On landing in Kenya, it was a humid but bright morning.

"Tam," the customs officer said.

I looked at her. She looked back at me. Then, I looked up, wondering if my cavalier, *Let's-get-a-visa-at-the-airport had finally landed me in trouble.*

"Huh?" I said for the fourth time.

"Tam!" she repeated.

I looked at Cadette, she had reached the front of her line and was now next to me. I stretched out my palms helplessly.

"Taaaaam!" the customs officer was now getting impatient.

"Oh, thumb!" Cadette finally said.

I started laughing, then realising I didn't know if the customs agents here had no sense of humour like the ones in Lagos, I quickly put my fingers on the wet panel and off we went.

It was clear I needed to get used to the cadence here.

My first stamp. In Africa. As an African.

The airline organised a bus to take us to the hotel. We boarded but the bus did not leave for another hour and nobody told us why. It made me feel right at home. This is just like Lagos.

It was 6 A.M. The heat of the morning was starting to rise off the tarmac, just like I was used to. It was so hot, you could bake bread in the air.

There was also a familiar smell that gave me comfort and a familiarity with the way people moved. There was no rush, they were lackadaisical about almost everything, and most of all, they were warm and hospitable.

The highway was dusty but it looked and reminded me exactly of Lagos. Lots of people heading to work. Some skipping over the motorway mid-thigh barrier, which was there to prevent exactly that sort of jaywalking.

At the hotel, more waiting, and then they served us breakfast. It was the most delicious thing I'd ever tasted, especially the succulently sautéed mushrooms. Cadette and I couldn't stop eating it.

After my third go-around at the buffet, Cadette turned to me and said, "This is not mushroom, it's liver."

I calmly finished my third plate.

After a nap, the first thing we wanted to see was animals.

So we asked where the nearest safari was, not knowing safaris were usually way out of town in the mountains or in uninhabited places.

Someone told us about an orphanage for animals rescued from the wild, and that they had lions.

That'll do, so off we went.

I've never seen so many loose monkeys in one place. My primary school in Nigeria did have a monkey that I would see occasionally but that's a story for another day.

Back to the Kenyan monkeys, there they were, randomly displaying their bums and baring their teeth. After I laughed at one particularly amorous male, he turned around to chase me on the open road by the turnstiles.

After a while, it was clear we were the only ones left in the park, but the guards were in no rush. In fact, they subtly asked us for a bribe, calling us their beautiful

African sisters, and promising they could get us even closer to the animals, and they did.

It was wonderful and worth it.

My first bribe.

We took selfies with the lions, got to stroke the cheetah and chatted with our African brothers. On the floor of a shaded area, was this skull of enormous proportions. It had been there so long that it had been stripped white by the elements and bits of rock and red mud covered its nooks and cracks. Nobody could tell me which animal it was from – their best guess was a rhino.

The sunshine in Nairobi is unparalleled, it makes the skin glow. I needed no make-up, and the selfies turned out well.

After our adventures with the wild orphans, we headed to the hotel where we saw on TV that Fidel Castro had died. All talk was of how he was a hero of Africa and helped with the cascade of African independence in the early sixties, starting with Ghana. Quite the opposite to what we had been told in the West. I guess history favours the person with the longest pen.

Welcome to Guangzhou

The next morning, it was time to leave Nairobi but we did not mind. We had more adventures in Mozambique.

I knew nothing about Mozambique and that would soon be to my regret because we were held for four hours at the border. More about that later.

The bus back to Nairobi airport was due to leave our hotel at 11 AM but at noon, we were still waiting for one more passenger to board.

I turned around to make chit-chat with some people on the bus. Most were connecting to Guangzhou. *How exciting*, I thought jealously.

"What are you going to do in Guangzhou?" I asked one of my fellow travellers. She was Nigerian.

"To shop," she answered. "I'm a trader."

I realised after our chat, Guangzhou had become the new Dubai for Nigerians. Making round trips to buy and sell things for a premium "*Made in abroad*" prices back home. I was impressed but wondered what that was saying about the sea change back home. On one hand, I loved that the world was becoming smaller and people thought nothing of hopping on a plane to China, whereas a decade before, the obsession had been with Europe and sometimes, Saudi or Dubai.

After what felt like hours, a Chinese guy rushed out of the hotel clutching several bags. When he boarded our bus, everyone yelled at him for holding us all up. I watched with second-hand embarrassment but I also hoped that his English was limited and all the insults flew right over his head.

Our departure from Nairobi was uneventful but I would come back to Kenya again two years later, being the place I found the most healing after the death of my mother.

The second time around, I went to Mombasa to spend time by the beach.

Mozambique

Fear and Loathing in Maputo

It is hard to overstate the whiff of oppression that eclipses Maputo, the capital of Mozambique.

From the skies, it was not obvious as the plane floated over the long coastal nation, but that was where our joy ended. I took pictures from the plane of the white sandy beaches, the red roofs, inlets of sea water and the bits of greenery dotted around the busy landscape.

As we landed, we were encouraged to take a card and fill them in by the waiting stands, then queue to get in. I overheard some Canadians as they filled in their forms. We had all come from Nairobi, I wondered idly what they had got up to in Kenya and what they were doing so far away from home.

As we got to the front of the queue, I started to notice that white people were being passed straight through easy and one-by-one, they funnelled most of the black people through to a bench by the side of the large, hanger-like airport.

"Wait over there," the guard waved vaguely to a bench outside a large office.

"Why?"

No response.

After about twenty minutes, I got up to go into the office we had been sitting outside of, to figure out what was going on and how long this endless wait would be.

What was inside can only be described as heaps and mounds of paper on a sea of tables, some covered in oil, possibly from lunch, and the woman who presided over it all, the face of Maputo, had even more mountains of paper in front of her. She looked like she had been poured into her uniform. She looked up, unimpressed and did not respond about why we were being kept outside and why no one was saying anything.

As I sat, I eavesdropped on the conversations around me in case this was some sort of African Guantanamo Bay and I was about to be rounded up straight to Kiri Kiri.[1]

Was something wrong with our landing card? Was there a visa issue? I thought this was a visa-on-arrival country.

There was a woman amongst us who lived in Maputo but her brother was being held on the bench and they wouldn't release him to her. So she sat with him.

There was a Nigerian guy who lived in China but had a connecting flight from South Africa – apparently something was suspicious about his layover so they held him too.

This third story I am unsure of, there was a Somalian guy, who was just sitting there, not talking to anybody. He was the least nervous looking there, like he was somehow sure of his future off the bench.

A guard occasionally took pity on us and updated us on things. "They've called the boss, he is coming soon."

Who was this boss?

Why was he coming?

---

[1] Kiri Kiri is a notorious prison in Lagos.

What was wrong with our papers?

Why are we being held?

Can we reboard and just go straight to Tanzania?

To the paper-hoarding woman, we submitted our trip plan through three countries – Kenya, Mozambique and Tanzania – to prove we had a return ticket. Something about this made them even more uncomfortable.

I went in to explain our professions to the lady, thinking the problem was our itinerary and they were worried we couldn't afford it.

She refused to engage or speak to me. A man would come by each time to usher me away and ask me to wait for the boss.

Amidst all this, Cadette was doubled over in agony because she had started her monthlies and we didn't have access to our luggage.

Every time we went in to speak with the fat gatekeeper, she would grunt and ignore us. We tried to ask for help for Cadette's period but they didn't help.

After four hours, the boss finally arrived, a rotund man in his sixties. He signalled for us to follow him. Then he stopped outside a door and said, "Wait here," signalling to Cadette, holding his palms out as if to stop her.

In his office, he sat for what felt like a quarter of an hour in silence then he calmly loaded up an old-school projector.

What ensued were passport pages projected onto the blank, white wall of his office.

At first, I didn't think it had anything to do with me so I paid no attention, I kept waiting for him to speak.

He's looking for something. More time wasting, I thought.

Then by the time I started paying attention, I caught the last slide. It was an Irish girl, and of course my eyes went straight to her age.

She was twelve.

The Boss looked at me.

"Are you being trafficked?" he said, without irony.

"Me?" I started laughing, then realised he was serious. "No!" I said, then repeated it again. "I'm too old to be trafficked."

"You will be surprised. What these girls have in common is that they were trafficked," he said drily.

That's when I put two and two together. Cadette and I didn't match the profile of travellers. Without make-up, we looked like teenagers and that definitely did not match the profile of travellers traipsing through three African countries.

"We can call my dad and you can speak to him. He'd be horrified you think I'm being trafficked," I reassured The Boss.

Shortly after, he let us go. I was still none the wiser as to why they held us at the airport.

We were exhausted by the time we left the airport. We took a taxi to our hotel, then we were transported by a golf cart in the dark to our hotel rooms.

We had exactly twenty-four hours left in Maputo and the airport ordeal had robbed us of any zeal to see the city.

The next day at breakfast, we were surprised to see all the senior staff at the hotel were white and the junior waiting staff were black. Something about it felt uncomfortable. We also witnessed some of the senior staff yelling at the junior ones for various things, which in the context of the colonial-looking hotel – thatched roof, vaulted ceilings and windowless expanse of outside space – made for uncomfortable viewing. The junior staff drifted about with their heads down, not making eye contact, afraid of their own shadow.

After breakfast, we took a walk by the sea, there were lots of palm trees lining the seaside and the highway. There was a fenced off area on a corner of the beach, where several young men stood idly by playing loud music and leaning on cars. It was not clear what was going on, if it was a party or a car wash.

We stopped off at a five-star hotel. The staff were mostly Chinese and everything – menu, signage – were all translated in Chinese. Welcome to twenty-first century Africa.

We headed to the rooftop to take photos until someone kicked us off because we weren't supposed to be on the rooftop.

After settling down into the lobby, Didier, a business man from francophone Africa, came to hit on Cadette. He took our numbers and talked about his life in South Africa. How much time he spent away from his wife and how life in South Africa was much better than in Congo.

After a while, Didier left and we contemplated crashing the wedding upstairs. I say contemplated, but the truth was I actually attempted to crash it, and could not find the entrance. You could see the wedding from the atrium and the entrance looked like it was on the second floor but it wasn't so I came and sat back down.

The next day, we left Maputo.

In trying to leave, it was the same story on the way out.

"You're going to Tanzania, you need a visa. So you can't leave," the customs officer said looking at me, stony-faced.

"But you said yesterday I couldn't come in," I said. "Which is it?"

No response.

I turned to the guy next to me for help. He shrugged at me helplessly, waved his Swiss passport, then muttered something in French.

Cadette was at a different desk, two officers away. I looked at her but it seemed she was having the same problem.

"Tanzania is visa-on-entry for British citizens," I said, but for all I knew, that wasn't what the officer heard.

I started to sweat, imagining the ordeal of the previous day happening again.

The Swiss guy went through.

This was a pattern we would come to observe later, like in Namibia, the queue with just white people seemed to move a lot faster, whereas if you were black, they looked at you with suspicion. *Why are you moving so freely through our country?*

I kept insisting to the officer I didn't need a visa to go into Tanzania but she didn't respond. I wondered if it would've been worse with my Nigerian passport, which incidentally, I had in my back pocket, in case things went sideways. I had read that you could also get a visa on arrival with a Nigerian passport into Mozambique so I brought it with me but I realised at this point, it may complicate matters.

Eventually, after repeating myself several times to which her response was mute grunts, she let me through.

It was only days later that we worked out no one at that airport spoke English and hardly anyone on the hold-up bench spoke Portuguese.

It was a language barrier problem. The racism stands but it was mostly a language wall.

Lusophone Africa is something that is barely spoken about. The atrocities of the French, the Belgian and the British left a larger imprint across Africa and is spoken about more than the Portuguese. It had not occurred to me that the official language of Mozambique was Portuguese.

If I had learnt even a little bit of history about Maputo, I would have known to be prepared for that waiting bench. It later occurred to me that they couldn't communicate with us.

I had other problems with my stay in Maputo. There seemed to be this atmosphere of fear everywhere. Employees were afraid of their bosses, people were afraid to make eye contact, choosing instead to mumble their words and try to escape as soon as possible. We saw this in our few interactions on the road side, the hotels and in restaurants.

Having said that, the Maputo seaside is beautiful. I enjoyed interacting with the many women selling fish by the roadside and watching the fish boats pull in as the sun set over the bright horizon.

Tanzania

Dar Es Salaam

To save money, we stayed in an Airbnb in Dar Es Salaam, the largest city in Tanzania. Most people think Dar Es Salaam is the capital because the international airport is there; however, it stopped being the capital in 1996 and that honour was transferred to Dodoma – a city I have never heard anyone even speak about.

We found a large, modern flat in the expat district to stay in. We entered through the multi-storey underground car park where several fancy cars were parked, then up the dark stairway into a huge apartment with rhythmic ceiling fans turning gently to stir the still air of the Tanzanian heat.

The host was a British guy named Nasser and we knew nothing about him except the word of Airbnb. Airbnb was in its infancy so Cadette and I joked but also plotted hypothetically how we would escape if Nasser turned out to be a kidnapper or worse. We didn't have to worry about that because when we arrived, he was out of town and we were greeted by his housekeeper, Esther. He left us helpful, extensive instructions which helped us to settle in.

I was not so interested in Dar Es Salaam as much as I was looking forward to our final destination, Zanzibar. We had booked a remote area of the island for some R n R.

The next day, we took a walk on the streets of Dar Es Salaam, it was mostly uneventful apart from the smelly ocean, which I can still smell in my memory whenever I think back to that day.

Dar Es Salaam looked like most major cities: cars, cabs, glass-fronted high-rises and business people bustling about. We walked in the direction of downtown with the vague aim of finding some food and drifted past two adjacent Chinese restaurants. A Chinese guy sat in front, wearing a white singlet and flip-flops, the uniform of idle, young African men, fanning himself under a Pepsi-branded canopy. He looked right at home.

Cadette and I looked at each other and laughed. He reminded us of the ubiquitous young guys in Lagos, sitting languorously in front of makeshift bukas[1], enjoying the afternoon breeze and incandescent heat.

After another hour or so of walking, we took a cab to a seafood restaurant, where I had some of the best fish of my life. The service was outstanding, the clientele were suitably posey and the view of the ocean was ridiculously beautiful.

After watching the sun set, we had some dessert and headed home.

On our last day in Dar Es Salaam before we headed to the island, we decided to explore the local markets. We had a sneaking suspicion we were being cheated when we asked for prices in our normal accent; figuring quickly we were tourists, traders would reach for ridiculous prices. So, we asked the housekeeper,

---

[1] A casual, cheap, makeshift restaurant, usually on road-sides.

Esther, to accompany us for the day so we could get the full Tanzanian experience.

"Hey bajaji," Esther would yell, to grab us a three-legged motorcycle.

Cadette looked at me – our first mistake, we'd been taking cabs instead of the bajaji. We squeezed ourselves into the makeshift cushions in the back of the pimped-up motorcycle, resting our heads under the hooded cover away from the midday sun.

After about half a day, Cadette looked at me again and in a dark, low tone in Yoruba, said, "I don't think she's haggling. She's just calling bajaji."

I realised she was right. There was simply no point to have carried this woman along during our whole day. We were just paying extra and getting the same deal.

She did take us to get some wonderful Tanzanian street food at the end of our day. I just remember piles and piles of delicious meat and rice.

The next day, we attempted the ferry to Zanzibar.

Chaos does not begin to describe the scene at the ferry station. First of all, the taxi did not get us there on time as we underestimated the traffic in Tanzania's most populous city.

Once we got there, we realised it was cash only to get tickets so we had to run around in the baking heat, looking for a cashpoint. I stood by the luggages while Cadette went searching for cash. I remember being overwhelmed, hot and paranoid. I was surrounded by men trying to sell me stuff, the noise and the heat was overpowering. By the time Cadette returned, I was yelling at the men hawking their wares, thinking they would get angry if I didn't buy something.

"Look at them, they're really gentle. Just say no," Cadette advised.

I looked up. She was right. These were no Lagos area boys. I took my head out of the perceived danger zone and looked each one in the eye and said, "No, I don't want to buy a coconut or a handkerchief. I don't need another t-shirt or sunglasses, thank you so much." Slowly, they drifted off and left us alone.

By the time we got to the ferry counter again, it had left. We bought tickets for a later one and went to sit at the top of a nearby hotel and watched the ocean from our vantage point.

The view was beautiful and the buildings around the port were very modern. The area seemed to double as the banking district as well as being the port.

The hotel restaurant where we sat was beautiful, and even though it took them forty-five minutes to make our food, it was the best salad of my life – cucumber seeds the size of diamonds. Heaven!

This is a running theme when travelling in Africa, how long the food takes to arrive in a restaurant. I see a lot of complaints about it in reviews but it gives me comfort the longer the food takes, because I think it means it is being made from scratch and not hustled out of the freezer and defrosted for patrons.

Around us and below, everything looked blue from the hotel balcony as glass-walled offices reflected both sky and ocean; we enjoyed fresh juice and batted off flies who tried to share our meal with us.

The Ferry

As we approached the ferry, dragging our suitcases and bags, at least three different guys came up to us saying, "First class?" and pointed helpfully to the front half of the ferry.

"No, we bought standard tickets," we responded proudly.

Why would I buy first class ticket? I scoffed, the difference was $15! Oh, and foreigners were charged in dollars while locals paid in shillings for the ferry.

As we stowed our luggage in the last undercarriage, we walked back to search for seats. We quickly realised, the "seat" sold to us was more of a suggestion. The ferry was completely overbooked and there were no assigned seats. There was a deck at the top where about a hundred tired-looking people assumed various uncomfortable-looking poses, ready for the two-hour journey.

After our ordeal of the afternoon, I was not about to stand for two hours in the baking sun, not after paying $35. So we went to look for someone who could upgrade us so we could actually be inside the ferry, sitting down.

"Sir," we grabbed a guy in uniform. "Can we upgrade to first class, please?"

"Wait here, I will come back," he said.

I looked at Cadette. Success!

He came back and said, "Follow me,".

Cadette nudged me for some cash so we could pay for the upgrade. She gave it to the guy. He pocketed it but did not provide a ticket in exchange.

Cadette looked at me. I shrugged.

Our second bribe.

"I guess there is no ticket window where you can exchange these useless, standard tickets," said Cadette.

Then what happened next was amazing. He took us to another part of the ferry. It was practically empty, air conditioned, there was even a TV. This was what I was expecting when I paid $35 for a standard ticket.

It was pure heaven and I promptly fell asleep. The next thing I saw when I woke up was Stone Town drifting by, the red-bricked archaeological town welcoming me to the historic island of Zanzibar.

Stone Town, Zanzibar

Ocean smells, acacia trees, spices, ships in the distance and colonnade houses built from stones, were the sites that greeted us as the cab pulled out of the ferry area to take us to Nungwi.

Nungwi is on the northern part of the island of Zanzibar and is untouched and very rural.

The architecture in Stone Town, by the docks, is borne out of the coral stone in the topography, so you have these tremendous buildings with tall, carved doors, with Arabic design influences, and it has become a world heritage site. It has to be seen to be believed.

The sun was setting as we pulled away and we observed a descending pyramid of kids just finishing off a tower of handstands – beautiful and a welcoming welcome to the island.

I'm glad to say Cadette caught this spontaneous pyramid on video, which I still watch from time to time and the sunset in Stone Town forms a part of the cover of this book.

The journey to Nungwi was just over an hour and our cab driver would occasionally wave to random people and say, "That's my son."

After the third time, I took the plunge and asked, "How many children do you have?"

"Six," he said without irony.

I think I laughed. No, I sniggered. But there was no follow-up laughter from him.

I thought he meant 'son', the way Africans loosely say, 'he's our son', when they really mean 'nephew' or 'little neighbour boy down the street'.

But he was not joking, those boys really were his sons.

He didn't seem to be offended by my snigger as he then gave us his card and promised he could pick us up again in a week's time when we were ready to leave.

The rest of our stay in Nungwi was uneventful. I made a friend on the beach in my quest to quench boredom, while asking for things to do apart from the moon party, which sounded like my idea of hell.

The friend, Florence, turned out to be Ugandan and I would later meet up with her some years later as I continued my sojourn through East Africa.

Asante Sana

There was something very odd about the staff of our hotel in Nungwi. Actually, there were several odd things.

First, was the fact that everything was priced in dollars which posed a huge disparity from the local currency, you can start to guess the extent of the rip-off that everything was. As the week went by, it started to grate on my nerves.

Cadette is an economist so she took care to explain why it is bad for an economy to spend other countries' currency – something to do with how it pushes down the demand for their own currency and devalues it.

The staff here, again, much like the ones in Mozambique were very subservient, not quite making eye contact, had switched off their personalities and were ruled by an iron-hand South African woman built like a shit-brick house. They responded to every question "Asante sana", meaning 'thank you' even when you were simply making an observation, which after my bizarre colonial experience in Mozambique, I was not in the mood for.

This part of the island though was beautiful and untouched. I came across a rudimentary boat one afternoon, just floating ethereally, out there in the middle of the ocean, you could see its jagged edges from the fresh carving, it was the colour of whitewashed wood from where the unvarnished surface had been bleached further by the Indian ocean. I took several pictures, there was something that touched me about the hard work of someone making that boat and probably using it to catch their daily meals.

One of the best conversations I had with one of the staff at the restaurant was with a young man, who went rogue one night and told us about his story. After hearing that they worked six days a week and lived locally in some hostel rather than onsite, and only got to see their families when they were rarely let off the island, I set about finding out more.

"Where are you from in Tanzania?" I said one evening to the whipper snapper.

Cadette rolled her eyes and I knew what that meant. I was being too nosy.

"I'm from Rwanda," he said.

"Wow, that's a long way away from home."

"Yes, my father escaped Rwanda during the genocide and crossed over to Uganda. That is how we ended up here."

Of course, during my cross examination, we were both on tenterhooks because even though it wasn't explicitly said, we knew that if caught during this casual conversation, the young boy would be in trouble and may lose his job.

"I'd love to hear more about your story, have you ever thought of writing about it?" I asked.

"No," he said and slinked off to the kitchen.

I wanted to know more, what that was like escaping the border, crossing several countries to Tanzania then over to this island to make a living. It was too awful to think about.

As an immigrant child myself, I sort of knew what that was like but our story involved planes and a plan. It wasn't a random fly-by-night over the border because the majority ethnic group had descended upon your minority group and wanted to decimate you and your family.

"Who owns this hotel?" I asked another staff member during another one of our expensive dollar-ticketed meals another evening.

"A South African," he said.

There was a theme here. It seemed the dark hand of South Africa extended far beyond its borders into other parts of Southern Africa. I wondered what else had extended?

Video Vixens

Coming back to Dar Es Salaam, Cadette wanted to revisit the fish restaurant, it was an outdoor restaurant built on stilts, with a terrace jutting out into the sea. Apart from the occasional smelly wave of fishy water, the view was spectacular and I was glad for a bit of sea breeze.

After a while of waiting for our food, a man appeared and plopped himself at our table but didn't say anything. He had dreadlocks, wore sunglasses, several gold chains and a sharp whiff of entitlement.

"Have they also given you this table?" I asked kindly.

He didn't answer. He kept his sunglasses on.

Genuinely confused, I asked him again why he was sitting at our table because we had this booked. There was no waiter around to offer an explanation about why we were suddenly sharing a table. The man didn't take off his sunglasses and he didn't offer any explanation.

Cadette was smiling through all this. Perhaps she understood the unspoken interruption better than I.

After a while of silent confrontation, he left and we could relax and eat our meal.

As the evening went on, I slowly became aware of a changing atmosphere around us.

After a while, a senior staff member came to our table. "Are you girls ok? I'm so sorry about this."

Then I realised what I thought was just general hum drum of background noise in the restaurant was Dreadlocks complaining about us loudly in Swahili with a smattering of English swear words.

I didn't speak Swahili so it took me a long time to recognise this.

Now paying attention, I could hear, "I make video vixens out of women. I could have made them video vixens."

As it turned out, he was a Congolese rapper and was famous in East Africa.

That was none of my business, don't plop yourself at my table, sir.

On reflection, I found the whole thing to be embarrassing, like I was the one who lost my social cues and sat on a stranger's table expecting them to worship me.

A Stranger's Pose

On the way home, the sun was setting so beautifully over the horizon.

It doesn't matter how often you see a sunset, there is still something transcendent about a clear mauve sky or the immersive yellow light that transmits from the end of the horizon towards you, signalling nightfall. I've always found it fascinating that as soon as that sun descends, which takes seconds, the night shade is immediate, you don't get a chance to reflect over what you've just seen, you are immediately dunked in darkness, and left with the memory of dusk.

Knowing I had seconds, I took out my camera wedged inside the tiny seats of the bajaji and started taking pictures of the sunset.

It was difficult, the bajaji was stuck in traffic, and the occasional drift of the tall buildings of Dar Es Salaam eclipsed my focal point. So I kept trying. Click! Click!

After a while, the bajaji driver said to me, those people by the side of the road are complaining that you are taking their picture.

I was surprised.

Not speaking Swahili, I didn't register the agitation happening yonder by the bajaji garage.

"No, I'm not taking their pictures. I'm just trying to capture the sunset," I responded but I stopped.

I suppose if you live in a place where the sunset is beautiful every night, and it perfectly reflects the red dust of Africa, you can take it for granted and wonder why a couple of tourists are staring intently and trying to capture it on their phones.

Part 2: South Africa, Namibia, Zambia, Rwanda and Uganda

South Africa

Winter, South of the Border

It was June. We wanted to start at the bottom of Africa and work our way up to the East in Uganda. We skipped Botswana and Zimbabwe, and two other places as well, Lesotho and Eswatini (known then as Swaziland), both landlocked countries within the behemoth of South Africa.

We landed in Cape Town and went straight to our Airbnb in Camps Bay.

The first thing that struck me was how cold it was and how the roads looked exactly like the Netherlands, where I had done a purgatorial stint as an expat.

The apartment in Cape Town was so nice. My memories of it are: it was right by the beach, modern and there was a pancake and ice-cream place nearby that delivered.

The first night was so cold that we struggled to stay warm and the cable TV was not working so I contacted, Gary, the owner to say, "Hey, oga, your cable is not working. Please pay the bill so we can watch E! channel."

He insisted it was working.

"But Gary it says here, pay for your subscription so you can watch this channel."

After several back and forths, he finally paid the bill and the TV started working.

A quick text to a friend revealed that it was winter in South Africa, being south of the equator, so everything was reversed compared with the global North.

Huh? I was genuinely shocked.

Part of my lack of awareness of living in Europe was knowing next to nothing about Africa and not realising there was winter. Africa is often painted as a utopic inferno. Even worse, was being African and knowing next to nothing about South Africa.

It is difficult to travel in Africa with an African passport. Colonial divvying up of the land had effectively kept Africans out but made sure Europeans were able to, not only get in and out, but also move around easily within Africa.

As we travelled up north, we realised it was also winter in Namibia and Zambia.

The next day we went to the cheapest shop we could find to buy sweaters. After that, we went to get pastries at the shopping centre, where this woman with her child pushed in in front of us, and when we tried to tell her, her attitude was you're in Cape Town, know your place. She was a white woman and there was a hierarchical way in the way she moved that signalled that we were the ones in the wrong. Cadette set her straight.

After that unpleasantness, we were done with South Africa, it was several things: the stares indicating that we did not fit into the landscape, the discomfort we felt when we went to restaurants and everyone sitting down was white and the waiting staff were all black, standing around awkwardly. If that happened in London, I'd be uncomfortable.

The flock of black people gathered at sundown waiting for the bus to take them back to their townships. It was like a scene from a colonial 1950s movie, except it was real and it was happening, every night. I wondered why friends who had gone to Cape Town, reported how great it was and did not feel uncomfortable.

But then, I always think of racism as something that if you're not the target, it is hard to see it. A bit like misogyny, a man cannot attest to another man's lack of misogyny, because he's not the target. He may inherently be treated differently by that man.

The bizarre happenings continued at a local pancake place with service at the bar, we waited ages to be served even though there were fewer than three people at the bar, but when an older, white couple came along, the server perked up and served them swiftly. Cadette and I looked at each other, baffled. The server was black.

A visit to Cape of Good Hope revealed that penguins could live and thrive in Africa, a continent known for being really hot and intuitively uninhabitable for such wintry creatures. A stage-loving penguin took a shine to Cadette and followed her around the enclosure, she named him 'fame whore'. After a while, he toddled off to join the others and we left the beach.

We ran into a white mother and daughter from Johannesburg who were so lovely and happy to meet Nigerians, they asked us how we were finding Cape Town and buttressed our sense that it remained racist and segregated. They assured us Johannesburg was more multicultural and we would not have experienced the same problems.

A highlight of our trip was Table Mountain; it was magic.

My favourite memory was on the way out a pictorial compilation of the other six wonders of the natural world including the Amazon, Halong Bay in Vietnam, Iguazu falls in Argentina/Brazil, Jeju Island in South Korea, Komodo in Indonesia and Puerto Princesa in the Philippines.

I've had the pleasure of visiting Halong Bay and although I was sick the entire time with food poisoning; being amongst these natural wonders proffers an ethereal state of being, like you're part of something supernatural, or maybe that was just my diarrhoea.

Namibia

Dry Ground and Springboks

The first thing I do when I enter a new country is ask "How much is a loaf of bread in the local currency?"

I do this for two reasons: to gauge how expensive things are in a country and to see how much cash I should take out for the duration of my journey.

If a loaf of bread is a tiny fraction of what I pay back home, then I know this is a cheap country and I can go wild. If a loaf of bread is twice what I pay back home then I know to be cautious, this is an expensive country.

My mistrust was at an all time high by the time we entered Namibia, although I struggle to remember why now. We had just received some crisp Namibian dollars at the cash point at the airport and I decided, for no discernible reason, that we couldn't accept lifts from any of the young men at the airport.

"We have to find the official taxi rank," I said, like I had been here before.

"Ok," Cadette said gently.

After half an hour of refusing lifts and perambulating Windhoek airport, we still had not secured a lift. I approached a family and asked them how they were planning on reaching their destination and were taxis safe even though there wasn't an official rank. They said yes.

So I thought, if it's good enough for this random family…

The youth that picked us up was a student, home for the holidays from America. He was very pleasant and drove us safely to our hotel.

There is one word for Windhoek. Dry. And not just because it was winter in July. The terrain was dry and for miles, all you could see were crisp, auburn tones.

Here was the capital of this southern African nation, the only thing I knew about it was that it was malaria free.

The roads were beautifully paved and the signs were in German and English.

I perused the menu at the hotel. More German.

The next day, we set out to go to the national museum, but it looked more like a taxidermist's office. Dank, dark and full of dead creatures. There was a skeletal staff of fewer than five, no other visitors and the exit took us into a dead road where it was impossible to flag taxis.

On the way home, we decided this city was not going to be the wild ride we had anticipated.

Quite simply, a safe, prosperous, functioning African country was boring. Contention was what made countries inherently exciting, I decided. Who hasn't walked down a street in New York and laughed at someone having a conflict-ridden conversation on the phone? Windhoek was not that. It was safe and predictable.

"Ok, let's book a safari," I announced one morning.

We called the hotel reception and very quickly they arranged a day-trip safari for us. They instructed us a driver would come, stop off at a safari ticket office in town, and we were to pay him the equivalent of several hundred pounds and we would be driven to the park.

Seemed simple enough.

It was our first safari and we were excited. Downtown Windhoek reminded me of any city in Africa – lots of the same banks and high-rise insurance companies.

The driver dropped us off and waited outside while we went to pick up the tickets. We entered a large but narrow office with tables arranged in T-shapes all the way to the back. A woman who sat facing the door greeted us when we came in. There was another younger lady sitting towards the back on the left. As we introduced ourselves that we had come to pay for the safari, "Oh, it's you two sisters," she said, like she knew us already and laughed.

Instantly, she dropped the price.

I looked at Cadette and we reached for the money and paid the significantly reduced price.

It was going to be a great trip!

The driver was supposed to get his cash from what we had paid the safari office so I thought we'd better inform the driver that his fee has been reduced and he should work it out with the safari lady – now known fondly as Auntie.

We went back outside and informed the driver. He scurried inside and came back out smiling. We're good to go.

On the way to the park, he stopped off and randomly picked up another man, who had halitosis so strong, he changed the chemical composition of the car. The driver did not explain, before or after, who this new man was.

After we got out safely at the park, Cadette said, "Why is it you're always sleeping when I'm convinced we're being kidnapped?"

She did not appreciate I had been knocked out cold by the sulphuric breath and I slept through it all.

There is a strange phenomenon called escorting that happens in Africa. That man may have been his cousin or his nephew. Often when you get a job or cash-in-hand gig, it is incumbent upon you to call a family member to escort you or come and watch you as you do this thing. That is just the African way.

To explain would have just led to more questions. How would that go?

"Hello girls, this is my cousin. I am going to pick him up and he is going to escort me to this park that is three hours' drive away."

That would not have gone down well with a couple of tourists.

The interesting question though is would he have done that with a couple of white female tourists?

The park had a lot of warthogs, a magnificent crocodile, a huge white rhino that almost toppled our Jeep and several other unremarkable animals. We were told the white rhino, hunted for its horns, was almost extinct and was one of the last remaining ones in Africa. Our driver, not the louche one from the morning, but the park driver, pointed out two men nearby, brandishing shotguns, who were hired full time to protect this one white rhino. Apparently, their chief enemy were Chinese poachers, helped out by corrupt local people. I didn't like seeing guns so up close, I looked around to see if there were any poachers hiding in the long grass around us.

There was a lone elephant who had lost her child recently. She moped around sadly around a decimated tree, with her trunk suspended at an angle. The driver explained that the elephant had gone on a destructive rampage after her child died that they'd had to cut some of the tree branches around her because she was destroying everything. I looked at the elephant for a long time, feeling her pain, and sometimes I still think about her. She was very sweet.

The driver further explained they were going to import a husband elephant from Tanzania or somewhere like that to keep the elephant companion. I didn't know they could do this. It was very fascinating.

On the way out from the park, now back in the taxi, there was a rather lithe ostrich that ran away from us as the radio played beautiful Namibian music.

One thing I noticed as we were back in the taxi heading out was that, we were still seeing more animals, like the ostrich, who was beyond the main gate of the park. There was no strict enclosure around the park and I wondered how they kept the animals in. Then I reasoned that, there was no incentive for the animals to really leave the park.

On the way home, the driver played Whitney Houston as the sun set on the dry Windhoek horizon.

It seemed our hotel doubled as some sort of show-off business breakfast place because the next morning, it was filled with Namibian business men, talking loudly and enjoying the Germanic breakfast offerings.

One of the men, pumped full of self-importance, was having breakfast with a colleague. He drank tea with his pinky up and wore the pointiest shoes I have ever seen.

He got up and on his way to the toilet, he slipped on the polished floor. It had Cadette and I in stitches. A complete splat. There was nothing left.

Our flight out of Windhoek the next day was at the crack of dawn. As we approached the airport, we saw the winter sun rise slowly from the blood-orange horizon.

I have fond memories of Windhoek and I had planned to do more. I had the contact details of a woman, who was the subject of a film I'd seen at a documentary festival, who told me I had to visit the dunes that edged the desert around Namibia. But when we got to Windhoek, not only was she out of town, the desert seemed like a long drive away so we left it.

The documentary was about how Germans had raided and pillaged a village in Namibia and stolen the skulls of the Herero tribe for scientific exploration, and the fight to get the skulls back.

Zambia

Kwacha in my Pocket

As we drove into central Lusaka, I noticed a ubiquity of billboards in Chinese announcing various construction projects along the highway.

Hang on, this looks familiar. I had seen this in Tanzania, the year before.

I proceeded to quiz our taxi driver on how the Chinese economic investment or colonisation, was being received by Zambians.

At that time, Nigeria had not yet undergone this "investment" as much as East Africa had.

The cab driver gave me the impression that it was a mixed bag. He was not particularly happy that Chinese companies brought their own staff and were not really employing locals for the plethora of construction jobs.

"Why don't the locals learn Mandarin?" I asked.

"They have. Some of them have," he answered.

It seemed that integration was not the aim of either the government or the foreign companies.

But that was just one guy's opinion. Time will tell.

"Why is everything so expensive here?" Cadette asked him.

The cab fare we negotiated was expensive and we found the currency confusing. I remember the taxi driver attempting to explain it all.

The bills were in thousands: 5,000; 10,000; 20,000; and 50,000 kwacha notes, which the government put in place as a result of inflation. Then later, the government "rebased" the currency, dividing denominational values by 1,000 so that a 5,000-kwacha bill became equivalent to 5 new kwachas.

In practical terms, this meant that smaller things that are usually cheap, like bread etc, would cost a big bill rather than a small bill/coins (since there were no longer any small bills). Pardon my rudimentary explanation, I am not an economist.

Let's Stay in a Nice Hotel

It was La Cadette's last country travelling with me, so we decided to treat ourselves to a nice five-star hotel in Lusaka.

The hotel was nothing short of glorious although we noticed the guards at the gate only opened the barrier when they saw white people approaching. When we approached, they left the gate and we had to squeeze ourselves through the smaller entrance on the side. This happened multiple times enough to confirm the pattern. The remnants of the brainwashing of colonialism was still alive and well in parts of Africa.

Whistle While You Work

I had been gone for a while so I decided to login and work remotely from the hotel.

I was talking to a colleague in India.

"Uhm, Lola, where are you?"

Not wanting to reveal I was somewhere in the deep folds of Southern Africa, I threw the question back, “Uhm why?”

“Your wifi is really bad. I can’t hear you very well.”

“Sorry about that.”

They call this the business centre. How does anyone do business here?

Still, I was grateful for the lax attitude on the continent. The room was empty and no one had stopped me from going in. I felt that, there was always someone guarding every corner of London and making sure people don’t have access to things, even if it is something as stupid as a seat in a lobby or business centre.

The Sichuan Experience

Having spent the better part of the afternoon lost within Lonely Planet forums, I found a recommendation for a Chinese restaurant. They had me at “authentically spicy Sichuan”.

“There’s a huge Chinese community here. Let’s try and find Sichuan food,” I said to Cadette, licking my lips in anticipation of the three-layered numbing chili I was so addicted to.

“Ok,” said Cadette, although she was ever the doubter of trying new things.

The walk there, to say the least, was scary. There were no street lights so it was pitch black apart from the occasional car headlights that drove past. It did turn out that the restaurant was at the back of a warehouse, as per the description.

We followed the pungent chili smell.

There was a local guy who worked there who can only be described as culturally Chinese. His cadence and way of speaking English sounded like he was speaking Mandarin.

"Have you spent time in China?" Cadette finally asked him one day.

"No," he answered politely.

"No? Do you speak Mandarin or Cantonese?"

"Small, small," he said. Then he bowed and backed away from our table with his head somehow still bent.

There was a Chinese woman behind the main counter, who we were convinced was some sort of Madam. Men would come, sit at the bar, chat to her for ages while she counted huge wads of cash.

That first day, at the end of our meal, it was hard to get a cab back to the hotel, no one knew where this restaurant was or maybe they didn't want to come out to this hidden warehouse. So we trekked home each time after a hearty meal.

We ended up eating there a few more times, until it got too much. Salt or sugar overload aside, it was the best Chinese food I've ever had on the continent.

Safari

"Mr Mwanza, what time is di tor?"

That was my attempt at a Nigerian accent. We had managed to get the number of a local driver to take us on safari.

I could not stop laughing. The deceit was killing me.

"Give me that!" Cadette took the phone off me and haggled successfully with Mr Mwanza to take a couple of Nigerian sisters on safari. Having learnt from our experiences in Namibia, we wanted the African rate, not the exorbitant rate he gave to white tourists.

"Ok, I will pick you up tomorrow at 7 am," he said.

The car had an inexplicable step inside, lining the front of the back seat, which made it hard to know where to put your feet. The step faced the wrong way too, so it did not elevate your feet but somehow you were leaning your shins against a large backward step. It was covered in thick, grey, dusty carpet, and if you moved your shoes even slightly, it awoke a cloud of dust. There was nowhere to hide.

"This road is really bad," I said after 20 km of relentless bumpiness.

"No, it's the car," Cadette said dryly.

By this time, I'd forgotten to hide my accent. It kept dropping. I wondered if Mr Mwanza noticed.

We were excited to see lions so we dressed up that day.

This safari was a gimmick at best. I thought Mr Mwanza would drive us around but when we got there, it was a shared safari with about twenty-five people squeezed into a modified bus, not even a Jeep, and you could not see the driver let alone the lions.

There was an inexplicable horse ride offered along with the day's events, which with our sandals, was not an enjoyable accompaniment.

After a couple more hours of disappointment, we called Mr Mwanza to drive us back to Lusaka.

More Chinese food.

Mr Africa

It was our last night in Lusaka. Cadette was going back to London and I was headed for Kigali and Kampala, the last two legs of my trip.

I was trying to get in touch with an old friend, Pieter, whom I knew when I lived in Amsterdam. He had promised me I could stay at his place in Kampala while he was out of town in Washington D.C.

While I wasn't going to Kampala yet, I would be there in a week and I wanted to make sure his place was still available.

I was running out of money and I needed to know it would be okay to stay at his place since it would save me a lot of cash.

He was not responding.

Rwanda

Nairobi is a huge hub in Africa so our flight from Lusaka took us there first. Cadette and I were to part ways here, I was heading for Kigali and Cadette back to London.

There were two queues in the connecting hall; I said goodbye as we joined our diverging queues. I had been travelling three countries with Cadette and it was now time to go out on my own. I could feel my shattered nerves, and honestly, I was a little sad too.

It was the middle of the night but the airport was far from quiet as everybody criss-crossed for their flights to various parts of the world.

In Kigali, I would be staying the first few days in a hotel and the last few days with a local Airbnb host.

I knew nobody in Kigali, what was I going to do when I got there? What would Rwanda be like?

Malaria

That first night in Kigali, I walked up the hill to a nice restaurant and got some delicious fried rice there.

A few nights later, I found out that this was a bad idea because people apparently got regularly murdered on that hill, or so my Airbnb host later told me. There was a convenient marsh next to it that murderers made use of to dump the bodies.

I definitely did not imagine that sleepy Kigali would have its own homicidal hill.

Indeed, the first word that comes to mind about Rwanda's capital is sleepy. It is quiet and the people are very gentle.

I woke up after my first day and went to the gym and ran for an hour. It felt great.

By that evening, I was deeply feverish and thought I was going to die so I called reception.

They called me a cab to take me to a local clinic. It was the weekend and very late at night so not many doctors were available.

I saw a medical student who took my blood and told me they would do a rapid test to see if I had malaria.

At this point, I started to regret the hubris that made me think I could travel through Africa without anti-malaria pills.

I had taken a yellow fever vaccination but no more, and that was because I needed a yellow fever passport to enter Uganda.

The "rapid" test took hours so I sat on the floor of the empty clinic, texting my family to let them know I may not be ok.

The medical student came back one more time, at which point I begged her to tell me the result of the rapid test.

"Only the doctor can tell you the interpretation," she said kindly.

I was desperate.

I didn't want to be sick on my own in a strange country, struck down with malaria with no one to take care of me. *What if I forget to eat and die alone in my three-star hotel on murder hill?*

My mind reeled with the various tragic ways this could end.

I even offered her a bribe, which she refused, to my shame.

My third almost bribe.

After another hour, the medical student came back and called me in to see the doctor.

The doctor turned out to be a pervert and tried to help me insert the thermometer through my bra into my armpit. Nice try.

"No, I know what axillary temperature is. I can do it myself," I insisted, snatching back the thermometer.

He sat down, visibly annoyed.

At this point, it must have been about 2 am.

He confirmed I did have a fever but it was not from malaria.

Crisis averted.

"Are you on your period?" he asked.

"No, I'm not," I told him.

I left and luckily the cab driver was still waiting for me.

I went home and started googling.

Turned out my one-hour session in the windowless, basement gym had dehydrated me to the point of a fever.

The Lord Speaks Kinyarwanda

I saw a sign for church in the foyer of the hotel so I decided to attend. It took place in the basement next to the gym that had almost killed me a few days before.

After drinking a gallon of water, I headed to the basement.

I was not prepared for a service conducted entirely in Kinyarwanda. I did not understand a word but I stood when they stood and clapped when they clapped.

I noticed they tried to engage me by looking at me and smiling, which made me feel undeserving of any special attention. How did they know I was not Rwandan?

After service, the pastor invited me over to her house. She had six children. I think their father had passed away.

The flat was in a poor area of town but it was elegant and well decorated. I was impressed with how the kids ran around preparing lunch and generally being hospitable and kind.

We had the most delicious spaghetti and a tremendous fruit salad with a side of avocado.

So this is what food tastes like without chemicals.

After lunch, she told me about her side business of running a bookshop. Then she took me to see it, I was surprised, it was not next door but rather a twenty-minute ride. We spoke at length about politics (she supported Paul Kagame), women's rights and the history of Rwanda. She told me that more than fifty percent of the ministers in Rwanda were women.

It was almost 4 PM, I needed to go back to my hotel but I didn't want to be rude. She was my ride, I had no idea where in town I was at this point.

Then she introduced me to another man at the business complex, I forget what he did for work. After a while, I did have to excuse myself and say could I kindly get a cab back to my hotel? She said no problem and actually dropped me off. She said she hoped to see me again at the next service.

I did not mention I was moving out to my Airbnb the next day.

Mr Laisser Faire

The first thing that hit me at the Airbnb was the wall of mosquitoes waiting at the door, when I got to the host's place.

The second thing was the noise.

Because of the lack of air conditioning, the windows were left permanently open, which allowed the thumping bass of Rihanna's *Wild Thoughts* to stream through the window all night from the club down the hill. If you know that song, you are familiar with the deep bass but little did I know it would be my soundtrack to Africa for the rest of the summer.

My host was supposed to be a couple but when I arrived, it was a lone man. He was nice, if a little cavalier with everything.

"Where is your girlfriend?" I asked him.

"She is studying in America," he said casually.

"But isn't she your co-host here?" I said, thinking I wouldn't have booked this place if I'd known I'd be sharing with just a man.

The next day, I got a text message from Pieter.

Pieter: When are you coming to Kampala? I'm back from D.C.

Me: Friday. Can I still stay at your place when you leave for Congo?

Pieter: Come here early, I want to see you.

Me: My flight is not until Friday. I want to explore Kigali first.

Pieter: Kigali is boring. I should know, I've lived there. Come to Kampala.

Me: I can't. Besides, the tickets would be too expensive to change.

Pieter: No, it won't. Is it RwandAir?

Me: Yes.

Pieter: Call them, they'll change it for free.

Pieter was an old flame.

We had gone on this amazing date when our paths crossed one summer in Amsterdam and hung out casually that summer. It didn't turn into anything serious and shortly after, he moved to Rwanda for a UN job.

After he left, some mutual friends told me he had been asking about me. We kept in touch on and off over the years and the year prior to my African travel, we had another date in Amsterdam because he was home for the holidays.

We tried dating long distance that year but it ended in a break-up that Spring, until I ran into him again randomly a few weeks before my Africa trip. That was when he offered, well insisted, I stayed at his place on the Uganda leg of my trip. He said it would be better than an Airbnb. I said no but eventually reached out to him when I started running out of money in Lusaka.

At this point, Pieter had lived in up to four countries in Africa, thanks to his job in international development. His company was moving him yet again to Congo after an evacuation mission from South Sudan, when it erupted in a civil war. They stationed him in Uganda, to wait out his next post. They gave him a flat in Kampala, which he was intending to keep as a base while he worked in Congo.

Me: I managed to find a flight. You were right, it was free but it's not till Thursday.

Pieter: That's a shame. That's the day I leave. You're going through Kigali airport right?

Me: Yes, Thursday morning.

Pieter: Me too. I have a layover for a few hours before I connect to

```
Congo. Let's meet for coffee and I'll
handover the keys.
```

Blackout

I had some work to finish so I found a co-working space and took a cab there.

Kigali is a city of hills, very modern and clean with beautiful roads.

After about an hour at the co-working space, there was a blackout. A handsome Rwandan guy mentioned there was another co-working space on the other side of town which still had electricity so he offered his car and took us there. There were about four of us – a mixture of expats, locals and me.

I made some friends at the new co-working space and decided to visit the genocide museum with one of them the next day.

My new friend was a Singaporean-American named Laura; she worked at the World Bank and was on a work trip in Rwanda. It was quite exciting to meet someone who worked for such a mysterious and intangible organisation.

I learnt a lot at the genocide museum, especially the arbitrary nature of xenophobia and the power of forgiveness. It is the only genocide I'd heard of where forgiveness was the main tool for reparations.

That's a novel idea, I thought. *How about we apply that to other mass egregious acts committed by human beings everywhere?*

There were rows and rows of graves and at the end of the museum, a video of reparation and apology from the perpetrators to the victims.

Rwanda is a country of one tribe, which if you know Africa well, is rather rare. Yet, during colonial times, the people were divided arbitrarily according to the number of cows they owned into two tribes: Hutu and Tutsi.

During an uprising, the Hutus, on the government's urging, murdered about one million Tutsi people. It is sobering but also astonishing because those two "tribes" live side by side today in harmony.

As a result of the reparations, Rwanda is today a peaceful country to the point of being boring.

In the gift shop on the way out, I bought a kitenge-cloth laptop bag. I don't really like the kitenge cloth, or Adire as it's known in Nigeria, ever since I found out it's origins. Apparently, it was created by the Netherlands for its colonies in Indonesia, who in turn rejected it, and somehow it ended up on the shores of Africa.

My new friend, Laura, invited me to meet another friend, Mito, who worked for the Japanese embassy in Rwanda. They had met in Washington D.C while both working at the World Bank.

Mito's apartment was in a very posh area of Kigali and we took the darkened stairwell to the fourth floor to enter into this beautiful apartment with cream-coloured tones.

Mito loved Africa, to the chagrin of her family and friends, who did not understand her preference for Africa. By the time, I met her she had lived and worked in Ghana and was looking for a way to convert her temporary job at the embassy into a permanent one. She had a crush on a guy at the embassy, and was looking for a Rwandan boyfriend because as she told me "they were so nice". From what I had seen so far in Kigali, I definitely agreed.

That evening, we got invited to dinner with some more friends of Laura from World Bank. We went to this chicken restaurant called Pili Pili. There was a French couple there who were quite snooty and didn't talk to anybody but the rest of the guys were very lovely. In retrospect, there may have been a language barrier with the French couple; the former official language of Rwanda was French due to their colonial past but at some point it became English. Some of the group were civil engineers working on a research project. Everyone was doing something interesting that had brought them to Kigali.

After the lovely dinner, I said goodbye to my new friends. I was catching a flight to Entebbe early the next day.

Mito asked me to come back to Kigali if things didn't work out with Pieter, because it was her birthday the following week. I promised I would.

I never saw Mito and Laura again but I still think of them fondly whenever I think about Kigali.

The Road to Kampala

At the airport the next morning, I tried to wall off my heart.

I checked in my luggage downstairs and went upstairs to the security floor. I knew Pieter would be there soon and I tried to steady myself for the impromptu reunion.

I left the security queue, I didn't want to miss him while stuck in the queue. Then I went to stand by the railings and peered downstairs to see if he would show up. I saw him right away. I backed away from the railings and made my way slowly towards the security queue again. Pieter bounded up the stairs, all 6 ft 2 of him, looking handsome at 6 AM.

"Do you want coffee?" Pieter asked.

"No," I said curtly.

After we sat down, he peered at me over his cup. After a while, he started telling me about the ins and outs of his flat. How to get in. Who the neighbours were and which days the cleaner visits.

We talked so much, the flight started announcing my name.

I wished him luck in Congo and went off to catch my flight.

Uganda

I Left My Heart in Kampala

The international airport of Uganda is not in the capital, Kampala, as you would expect but rather in the old colonial capital of Entebbe. It is a bit of a drive to Kampala and I hadn't planned how I would get there.

When I landed in Entebbe, it turned out Pieter had arranged a cab for me although he did not mention it when I saw him a couple of hours ago. How surprised was I when I got out and a man named Isaac was holding my name on a big card. I smiled.

It was late afternoon when I got to Kampala. I was preparing to go out and get some food when I heard a knock on the door and an attractive German called Stefan stood there.

He looked me up and down and I did the same to him.

Pieter had told him all about me and asked him to check in on me. Stefan also lent me his wifi dongle so I could contact home and not feel so lost.

The rest of the afternoon, texts arrived from Pieter telling me who I could contact for various things and a couple of phone numbers of friends I could hang out with, if I wanted.

That night, Stefan invited me over to his place to meet his friends and to generally hang out. I gladly accepted the invitation.

The group were very nice, there was a strong smell of weed. I don't know why I was surprised. This is what young people do in large cities. They invited me to Murchison falls that weekend. In retrospect, I wish I had taken them up on their offer that day, but I was too shy, I had just met them and I didn't think they meant it.

Or maybe my instinct didn't want to go. They were going to be sleeping outside and I hadn't warned my mama back home that there was a chance I'd be eaten by a lion.

A City of Seven Hills

Kampala is colloquially known as the city of seven hills: Kololo, Makerere, Mengo, Nakasero, Namirembe, Rubaga, and old Kampala hill.

Pieter's flat was on Kololo hill, which turned out to be the poshest area of Kampala, full of embassies and other government ministers. Pieter's flat was one amongst a row of bungalows, which had been built in the 1960s for foreign workers who came to Kampala to work in the energy section.

Uganda is indeed a special place, the Nile passes through it, and so does the equator, the latter meaning it doesn't really get winters unlike the countries below it. So I was glad to arrive after travelling through South Africa, Namibia and Zambia, which was still a bit nippy, even in July.

I settled in quickly, I got a SIM card at the mall and a dongle so I could get wifi in the flat. I planned to stay longer in Kampala, more than I had done in the other cities, because I had heard how nice it was.

Out of curiosity, I also wanted to visit some universities here so I could see how things were done differently or similarly especially in the Science faculties.

I visited Makerere University, reportedly the best in the country. I had been introduced by friends of Florence, whom I previously met on a beach in Zanzibar.

Queen of Katwe

One Sunday morning, I called an Uber but each successive one cancelled on me until finally, after half an hour, one eventually turned up.

The driver was very kind and when he dropped me off, said, "Why are you paying by card?"

"I don't know, that's the default in the Uber app."

"Kampala drivers don't trust Uber to pay them at the end of the month so when they see you're paying by card, they cancel."

Oooooooh, that's why I've not been able to get a cab all week.

"You have to click 'cash' in the app," he continued.

There's a cash option in the app?

"Thank you, sir," I said as I dashed out the door into church, making a mental note to grab a wad of cash later.

I made two new friends in church. One was a journalist called Bimbi, and the other a German girl, Adela, who worked for International Justice Mission.

Adela asked if I wanted to go and see the movie, *Queen of Katwe,* in a town, somewhere between Kampala and Entebbe. That sounded like a long cab ride. With the Uganda Shilling 4,000 to €1, I said no problem.

The show turned out to be at an outdoor cinema with the director present along with some stars from the movie, although David Oyelowo and Lupita Nyong'o were not present. However, everybody else was there, including the real people the movie was based on, and they had a Q&A panel afterwards.

It was incredible seeing Uganda through the eyes of the local film industry. Mira Nair, was also there, an Indian director who had made Uganda her home for more than two decades.

There is a large Indian population in East Africa, and because they don't tend to mix with Ugandans, it is hard to meet them organically unless you are part of that community.

On my flight home a few weeks later, I did spend time talking to a Indian-Ugandan gentleman and his son as they flew to UK for a family reunion. They had been in Uganda for two generations and for some reason, the rest of the family chose to relocate to England.

The Music of Water

"Come, let me take you to Sipi Falls," Bimbi said, my new friend from church last week.

"What is Sip-py?"

"It is a famous waterfall in the East of Uganda."

Why would I go see a waterfall? I thought.

"We'll take a taxi there. You'll enjoy it," she added.

"Ok," I agreed.

What I didn't know was that "a taxi" in Uganda is a public minibus, one of those ones shaped like bread that packs people in like sardines with some live animals thrown in.

Well, there were chickens on our bus but I *was* wedged in between three people in the front including a very wide man, all the way to Kapchorwa.

This may not sound so bad, but throw in the fact that Kapchorwa was a six-hour drive on a road so dusty, it felt like the Kalahari. I had one arm hanging out the window all the way there, for leverage and support, so I wouldn't get crushed.

Bimbi was doing me a favour by showing me her country so I tried not to complain, but when we got there, she then told me we had to stay in a cabin with no electricity and running water. The place was "eco-friendly."

But why does that mean we must live in darkness? I couldn't see my shampoo.

If you know me, you'll know I hate the word cabin and everything it entailed.

The cabin was completely blacked out on the inside. For what reason, I don't know. On the outside, it was built with wooden slats that looked like bamboo, although I'm no expert in wood.

There was a lovely veranda where I spent most of my time. I didn't like sitting in darkness, for fear of lurking snakes and shadowy beasts.

The best part of the cabin was that you could hear the continuous gushing streams of the waterfall nearby, and if you stood at the right angle, you could see it too.

I started to get excited.

Bimbi told me there was a village nearby we could observe the sunset.

Alright, let's go.

As we approached, there was a man standing in the general grassy area who then asked us to pay to see the sunset.

My eyes could not roll far enough in my head. But we paid the man and he let us pass.

It was a cloudy but beautiful sunset, that I still remember today. I also remember the cows we shared it with on the way there.

Bimbi told me that families in the area invested their wealth in a family cow and that was why there were cows randomly tied down in the town.

The next morning, we went down to breakfast.

The place was heaving with white people: Italians, Germans, Brits.

Are we still in Uganda?

Then they issued us with sticks.

"What's this for?" I asked.

"They're for hiking," the leader said.

Oh. My. Gosh. I was not prepared.

I tried to steady my mind and work out what else Bimbi had not told me.

I put on my trainers and work-out clothes and followed the Italians.

We walked through maize farms, coffee farms and then lettuce farms. It made me wonder, if coffee grows at such a high altitude, why is Italy famous for it? Does Italy grow coffee? I'll leave you to wonder about the historical divisions that also allowed Belgium and Switzerland, for example, to claim the throne of chocolate production when they didn't grow cocoa.

After about an hour, we saw the first waterfall. It was around 10:30 AM, the sun had risen just high enough and it bounced off the white gushing streams. Everybody was silent and all we could hear was the rhythmic sounds of rushing water.

I tried so hard to capture it on my camera but no picture could do it justice, it didn't fit in the frame. Even on video, the rushing streams still sounded better off camera.

"Alright, let's go," the guide said after a while. "There's two more!"

Two more.

I was sold.

I could not believe what I had just seen. On one part, it was scary, in that you had to bend over to observe the depth of the water as it cascaded off the mountain we stood on, and on the other hand it was so bright, and long and tall that you just wanted to stare at it forever. I could not believe there were two more.

The area was surrounded by vegetation, so green, it looked like a picture.

I looked at Bimbi and thought no wonder she wanted me to see this.

Uganda is a beautiful place.

After another two hours, we came to the bottom of another waterfall. The backsplash went on for about twenty feet, and even though I stood quite a distance away, my hair still got completely soaked. Not that I minded, I raised my stick in the air and got Bimbi to take a picture.

It was glorious.

After this, we stopped for lunch at a lone cafe.

I looked at my watch and thought, with the six-hour drive, how will I make it back on time to Kampala? It seemed the rest of our party were staying another night in Kapchorwa. I had to abandon the last waterfall.

I made Bimbi book us an actual taxi this time. I could not endure another bus trip again.

By the time we got to Kampala, as I lay down to sleep, I could still hear the music of the water.

I did go back to Uganda two more times after that, once to live for six months.

After a few more days in Kampala, I got another text from Pieter.

`Pieter: I'm coming back.`

`Me: Coming back where?`

`Pieter: To Kampala. I arrive Tuesday.`

`Me: What happened with Congo?`

`Pieter: There is some mix-up with my work visa. I have to come back while they sort it out so I cannot legally be in Congo.`

The first few days when he came back were quite peaceful. It was friendly between us. We could always chat, he was a good talker: conversations about politics, travel in Africa, God, books, and all the things we shared in common.

Then one evening I went to a bar to meet a new friend and asked if he wanted to come along. He said yes.

They played lots of Afrobeats and Wild Thoughts by Rihanna. We played pool and I won.

On the taxi home, he sat very close and put his hand on my knees.

Pieter was technically between jobs so he spent his days playing tennis and buying furniture for his house on Lake Kivu in Congo, to later be shipped by his company.

I looked up Lake Kivu so I could visualise where exactly he'd be staying: I found out that there were two countries called Congo: Congo-Kinshasa, colonized by Belgium, and Congo-Brazzaville (also known as Democratic Republic of Congo [DRC], colonized by France). Lake Kivu was in DRC.

He was buying a lot of patio furniture because apparently he was going to have a big terrace in Congo. I found myself jealous of all the earthy wooden furniture he was investing in. The living room was overflowing and had taken on an oaky smell.

One day I came home to hear Pieter on the phone, prattling on in French. Then he left the flat with the door wide open and walked to the top of the hill on the front yard and carried on speaking in French. I guessed the reception was better on the hill outside. I shut the door to keep the flies out but was secretly impressed his French was getting better.

He had been learning in the house, to prepare for his new job.

I had known Pieter for many years at this point, and had watched his French get better and better.

Party at Stefan's

Stefan, the next-door neighbour invited us to a party at his house one Saturday night. His girlfriend,

Selina, was back in town for a short break from studying in Berlin. Selina was half Swiss, half Ugandan and as it turned out was from Kapchorwa, the same area as Sipi Falls. She told me about her people a little bit, that they were a naked tribe. I told her I didn't see any naked people while I was there.

At some point, the girls congregated in the kitchen and grilled me about Pieter.

"What's going on with you two?"

"We've never seen him with a girl here."

"How long have you two been together?"

I told them how much I knew. It was a confusing situation. He told me he wasn't going to be here and all of a sudden, this visa thing has happened and he is back. One minute it was on and the next it wasn't. I couldn't keep up.

They warned me not to put my heart in it, that he had been really weird ever since he escaped from Sudan in the middle of the night to gunshots and that he mostly kept to himself. He may be a little traumatised that he had to leave his former job because of unrest.

The rest of the night passed easily but I kept their information about Pieter under my hat.

I met lots of colourful characters at Stefan's party but the group that struck me the most were the ones working in microfinancing.

"What is microfinancing?" I asked the diminutive American girl next to me.

"We lend money to market women at low interest rates to help them expand their business," she said.

"How much is the interest rate?"

"Typically, they're lower than the banking rates here so usually about three percent a month."

"What sort of things are they selling?"

"Tomatoes, bread, arts and crafts, sometimes clothes," the American responded.

It was a conversation that stayed with me afterwards. Three percent interest on a small loan seemed like a lot, that was an annual rate of 42.6% compound interest. *What was the mark-up the women were making on tomatoes and bread?*

Yet, I met a lot of people in my six months in Uganda, working in this unregulated industry, and they talked with pride about helping market women and doing charity in Africa.

Visit to Makerere

The next day, I visited Makerere University. I had a meeting set up with one of the heads of the Biomedical Sciences department.

When I got there, I waited two hours.

Time is a loose concept on the continent so I was not offended.

After a little while, the secretary offered to call him for me on his mobile.

"He said he's in a meeting at the Serena Hotel," she said.

"But we were supposed to have a meeting here. At 12," I said.

"We're not aware of any meetings at the Serena Hotel but he says you can come and meet him there."

I took my leave. I was not about to risk rape in Kampala, even if it was in a five-star hotel.

Bushwackers

"How long are you planning on staying in Kampala?" Pieter asked me one day.

"My flight is not till the third. Why?" I said.

"Because I think you may have to move out on Monday."

"What?" I dropped my corn on the cob. "Why?" I asked once I had recovered.

"I have to give up the flat. My boss is paying for my apartment here and in Congo and I tried to keep this flat as I wanted to keep coming back to Uganda but he says I can't." Pieter said.

"But you said I could stay here. I still have another week to go," I said.

I spent the rest of the week in a haze. I couldn't think. We tip-toed around each other. I felt destabilised. I had not expected it, not to mention staying at his place was a financial decision because I wouldn't have to pay for a hotel.

"Let's have fun this last weekend," he said.

So he took me to Kabalagala, apparently the soho of Kampala or the red light district, depending on whom you speak to.

We went to a Congolese club, which was simply glorious. I'd never seen men dance like that. Then Pieter told me about the Sapeur tradition of Congolese people where they dress in really dapper, old style colonial clothes. A way of reclaiming their identity and pride in themselves. Odd, but interesting.

It was a night of revelry and his friend, a Dutch guy and another lovely Ugandan girl came along.

On Sunday night, I moved out a day earlier than planned. Pieter seemed quiet and introspective that day. We had a lovely goodbye and I didn't see him after then.

I first moved into a neighbourhood that seemed close on the map but in fact turned out to be a suburb of Kampala, I left after two days, the cab fares to my co-working office were getting too expensive. After that, I found a hostel which was much cheaper and right in the centre of town. I got a non-sharing room and stayed there for the rest of my trip. It was a great hostel actually, lots of people from various corners of the world.

I can't talk about Uganda without mentioning the food, especially chapati. Because of the Indian population in Uganda, roti had made its way into the culture except the Ugandan version was sweet, made in doughy layers and fried three times in ghee butter. It's the most delicious thing you're ever going to eat. The street food version was sometimes made with an omelette rolled in and fondly called Rolex, presumably a contraction of "rolled eggs".

I indulged several times in chapati while I was there, my favourite haunt was Big Mama's, where I got the gourmet version from a nearby mall until one day Cadette said, "Big mama is gonna turn you into big mama!"

The end

Why can't Africans travel in Africa so easily?

Why can I get to more places visa free with my British passport than I can with my Nigerian passport?

Africa's richest man, Aliko Dangote, has said he needs 38 visas to travel within the continent on his Nigerian passport while many European nationals, waltz into most Africans countries visa-free.

I am grateful I was able to take these trips and I do not take it for granted but I also wish Africa was as open to Africans and Europe is as open to Europeans.

Acknowledgements

Thank you to my fellow caper and travel companion, Cadette, for allowing me to tell this story. Sorry about the mosquito bites.

Also by Lola R. Opeyemi

Wrap me in Trees

Torn apart by poverty and austerity in their home country, the Alejo family become divided across two continents for more than two decades.

Can this close-knit family reunite and make things work or will their forced expatriation drive them apart forever?

Wrap me in Trees is a story of love, hope and forgiveness and what it means to walk the line of an immigrant.

For more news on Lola R. Opeyemi, visit www.lolaropeyemi.com or follow @lolaropeyemi on Instagram.

Coming soon by Lola R. Opeyemi

The Secrets in the Walls

Manoah was one of the lost children of the foster care "farming" generation of the 1960s, given away by his Nigerian parents so they could pursue their dreams of a career in London.

But what happens when his foster mother, Mercedes, tries to keep him for good? And what about Ophelia Mayberry, the girl next door whom he falls for while he's living with Mercedes?

When a secret threatens to destroy the foster home and its residents, Manoah is forced to leave. But what happens to the love of his life, Ophelia, and the other children?

The Secrets in the Walls is a story of courage and what it means to love with your whole heart.

For more news on Lola R. Opeyemi, visit www.lolaropeyemi.com or follow @lolaropeyemi on Instagram.

Printed in Great Britain
by Amazon

24386453R00051